REMEMBERING SLAVERY

Also by Ira Berlin, published by The New Press

Slaves without Masters: The Free Negro in the Antebellum South

Families and Freedom: A Documentary History of
African-American Kinship in the Civil War Era
(co-edited with Leslie S. Rowland)

Also by Ira Berlin and Steven F. Miller, published by The New Press

Free at Last: A Documentary History of Slavery, Freedom,
and the Civil War (co-edited with Barbara J. Fields, Joseph P. Reidy,
and Leslie S. Rowland)

REMEMBERING
SLAVERY

AFRICAN AMERICANS
TALK ABOUT THEIR PERSONAL
EXPERIENCES OF SLAVERY

AND

FREEDOM

EDITED BY

IRA BERLIN, MARC FAVREAU,
AND STEVEN F. MILLER

THE NEW PRESS • NEW YORK
in association with The Library of Congress
Washington, D.C.

The publisher of *Weevils in The Wheat: Interviews with Virginia Ex-Slaves*, by Charles L. Perdue, Jr., Thomas E. Barden, and Robert K. Phillips (Charlottesville, Va., 1994) has generously given permission to use extended quotations from this copyrighted work. Reprinted with permission of the University Press of Virginia.

The portrait on the cover is of Fannie Moore, a resident of Asheville, North Carolina. Ms. Moore's interview appears on pages 132–34.

"Mother to Son," from *The Collected Poems of Langston Hughes,* © by the estate of Langston Hughes, reprinted by permission of Alfred A. Knopf, Inc.

PUBLISHED BY THE NEW PRESS, NEW YORK
DISTRIBUTED BY W. W. NORTON & COMPANY, INC., NEW YORK

THE NEW PRESS WAS ESTABLISHED IN 1990 AS A NOT-FOR-PROFIT ALTERNATIVE TO THE LARGE, COMMERCIAL PUBLISHING HOUSES CURRENTLY DOMINATING THE BOOK PUBLISHING INDUSTRY. THE NEW PRESS OPERATES IN THE PUBLIC INTEREST RATHER THAN FOR PRIVATE GAIN, AND IS COMMITTED TO PUBLISHING, IN INNOVATIVE WAYS, WORKS OF EDUCATIONAL, CULTURAL, AND COMMUNITY VALUE THAT ARE OFTEN DEEMED INSUFFICIENTLY PROFITABLE.

The Library of Congress is the world's largest library—an institution that serves as the memory of a nation and contains over 110 million items in all media, on all subjects, and from around the world, including written material in over 460 languages.

The sound recordings of former slaves featured in this product are from the collection of the Library of Congress Archive of Folk Culture. The photographs of former slaves are from "U.S. WPA Records: Ex-Slave Narratives" in the collection of the Manuscript Division of the Library of Congress.

Smithsonian Productions is the electronic media production center of the Smithsonian Institution, the world's largest complex of museum and research facilities.

PRINTED IN THE UNITED STATES OF AMERICA

9 8 7 6 5 4 3 2 1

CONTENTS

FOREWORD

Racial slavery has shaped virtually every aspect of our nation's history. Slavery provided one of the essential legs upon which modern capitalism was built. Slavery shaped the development of the American political structure, from its peculiar form of federalism to the astonishing, and continuing, disproportional influence of Southern legislators. Today's various racial constructions—whiteness, blackness, and an Other category that persistently renders nonwhites and nonblacks invisible—are obviously rooted in the history of slavery and Jim Crow.

Enslaved Africans and their descendants were and are assigned the impossible role of maintaining stable American race relations. Slaves were instructed on pain of injury not to protest an unhealthy relationship fixed by whites for the benefit of whites. Remarkably, slaves did not obey. They managed to bring on the Civil War; in the process, they destroyed the system of slavery and delivered a more fully realized American democracy.

Those heroic people are the generation most represented in this important book-and-tape set. Daughters and sons of Africa, these children who bore the mark of the lash wanted free universal education for everyone, the right to vote for everyone, the right to own and work their land, the right to build communities, worship, and love each other without the threat of mob violence. The architects of a new nation . . . these are the people the Federal Writers' Project and others sought to restore to history during the 1930s and early 1940s. And these are the souls Ira Berlin, Marc Favreau, and Steven F. Miller want us to remember.

Those ex-slaves who lived to tell their stories do not all speak in one voice, nor do they share one big collective memory. The interviews do represent one of the few bodies of slave thought in which black slaves described the conditions they faced, their oppressions, their resistance. But some of the passages will frustrate readers interested only in dramatic cases of brutality or heroic acts of defiance. Alongside the tragic we find stories of "happy darkies" who virtually pine for the days of slavery, as well as detailed, moving descriptions of the day-to-day violence inflicted on the very young and very old.

Stories like the latter were told at considerable risk. As Wes Brady put it in his interview, "Some white folks might want to put me back in slavery if I tells how we was used in slavery time, but you asks me for the truth." Readers must remember that when these interviews were being conducted, the stench of "strange fruit" still lingered in the Southern countryside where many of the informants still resided. In 1935 alone there were fifteen recorded lynchings, for which no one was prosecuted. Prisons and jails were populated with African Americans whose only crime was isolence, the most infamous case involving nine young men falsely accused of raping two white women near Scottsbooro, Alabama.

The ex-slaves had reason to be scared. Readers must also keep in mind that what the elderly informants remembered about the old times was being filtered through their present struggle to endure the Great Depression. They spoke with their heads and their stomachs: "We was happy," recalled Felix Haywood. "We got our lickings, but just the same we get our fill of biscuits every time the white folks had 'em. Nobody knew how it was to lack food."

But fear and Depression hunger alone do not explain the complicated character of their recollections. Slavery was a painful period, an era African Americans had been trying to forget since Reconstruction. Consider that many black churches worked hard to eliminate the "ol' spirituals" as a way of removing all vestiges of slavery from their cultural memory. The worst of the informants' slavery experiences may have been purged from their minds.

In any case, the moments of pleasure and happiness that the ex-slaves *did* remember, never celebrate the master class or endorse the system of slavery. Even as slaves, black people struggled to own their own lives; they turned the quarters and yards and woods into places of quiet contemplation or hideaway dens for party people. Later they recalled those good times and even expressed sympathy and kindness for their keepers. How could they not? How on earth could so many people held in bondage have survived slavery without humor, joy, love, good times, healthy relationships, a sense of self-worth?

If all of these disparate stories and diverse voices embody one single theme, it is humanity. Together the narratives reinforce the incredible ability of African Americans to maintain their dignity and self worth, to offer the rest of the world a model of humanity that could emancipate "free" people the world over, including their own masters, the overseers, and even the "paddy rollers" dispatched to hunt down runaways. The smartest slaveholders must have come to appreciate black humanity and its capacity for love and forgiveness—for those qualities are precisely what spared the lives of the "masters" and their families. It is our recognition of the ex-slaves' humanity that enables us to discard the false dichotomies of "Sambo" and "rebel" and see these amazing black survivors as complicated human beings.

—Robin D. G. Kelley

PREFACE

Remembering Slavery is a short book with a long history. First among its many progenitors is André Schiffrin, publisher of The New Press. In 1995, Schiffrin and Ralph Eubanks, director of publications at the Library of Congress, initiated a project to make available a book-and-tapes version of the audio recordings of former slaves dating from the late 1930s and 1940s. A year later, Schiffrin invited Ira Berlin of the University of Maryland to lead the project; Berlin in turn enlisted Marc Favreau, then beginning graduate studies at the university, to join him. Together they began the laborious process of transcribing and annotating the tapes at the Library of Congress, which had been copied from the primitive aluminum disks that had originally stored the former slaves' reminiscences. In this work they found indispensable the extraordinarily detailed transcriptions crafted by linguists Guy Bailey, Natalie Maynor, and Patricia Cukor-Avila. Professor Bailey, now a dean at the University of Texas, San Antonio, generously granted permission to use these transcriptions and offered his own expertise in interpreting him. For that we would like to thank him.

Coincidentally, Jacquie Gales Webb, the series producer of Smithsonian Productions (the broadcasting and audio reproduction arm of the Smithsonian Institution), had embarked on a similar project using the recorded ex-slave interviews. With the aid of the institution's talented technicians, the Smithsonian group had retransferred the collection from the original source disks at the Library of Congress and performed audio restoration. Not only were the remastered tapes easier on the ear, they also permitted more complete and accurate text transcriptions. The Smithsonian had been working with the Institute of Language and Culture in Montgomery, Alabama, which under the leadership of Project Director Kathie Farnell had received a planning grant from the National Endowment for the Humanities to develop a radio documentary based on the interviews and had independently gathered many of the linguists and social historians interested in the audio transcripts.

In 1997, the two groups who had been working independently found each other. Steven F. Miller, one of the consultants for the Smithsonian project, joined Berlin and Favreau on the book project, and the two teams struck an active collaboration, coordinated by Joe Wood of The New Press. The projects jointly agreed to supplement the recorded ex-slave interviews with the transcribed interviews with former slaves gathered in the late 1930s by the Federal Writers' Project. This book and the two-part radio documentary of the same title are the fruits of this collaboration. Our aim has been to create two distinct, but complementary works. Their subjects are closely related and their contents overlap somewhat, but each contains considerable material that is not available in the other. (A transcript of the radio documentary appears as an appendix.)

An undertaking such as this, involving artists, scholars, and technicians from four different institutions, is rife with possibilities for confusion and even gridlock. That it ran smoothly and on time is a testament to the staffs at Smithsonian Productions, The New Press, and the Institute of Language and Culture. At Smithsonian Productions, we wish to thank Paul Johnson, director; Wesley Horner, executive producer, Martha Knouss, marketing manager, and particularly Jacquie Gales Webb. Technical wizards John Tyler, audio production manager, and Todd Hulslander, production engineer, performed the remastering of the recorded interviews. At The New Press, Joe Wood helped to shape an idea into a manuscript; and Diane Wachtell, associate director, Grace Farrell, managing editor, Fran Forte, production manager, and Greg Carter, editorial assistant, helped transform the manuscript into a book. Kathie Farnell of the Institute of Language and Culture was instrumental in coordinating the various components of an enterprise that grew larger and more complicated as time went on.

Both the book and the radio documentary have benefited from the scholars who served as consultants: Guy Bailey; Richard Bailey of Montgomery, Alabama; Alwyn Barr of Texas Tech University; Jeutonne P. Brewer of the University of North Carolina, Greensboro; Horace Huntley of the Birmingham Civil Rights Institute; and Robert McElvaine of Millsaps College. Their criticisms and suggestions have been enormously helpful. Alan Jabbour, director of the American Folklife Center at the Library of Congress, and Joe Hickerson, the center's head of acquisitions, generously explicated the complex history of the Slave Narrative Collection after its accession to the Library. We would especially like to thank Jeutonne Brewer, who shared her unrivaled knowledge of the making and preservation of the recorded interviews and offered sensible suggestions about presenting them to an audience of general readers.

Like all modern scholars of slavery, we are indebted to the pioneering work of George P. Rawick and his associates, Ken Lawrence and Jan Hillegas, who brought into print the typescripts of the ex-slave narratives collected by the Federal Writers' Project. Thanks are due as well to Charles L. Perdue, Jr., Thomas E. Barden, and Robert K. Phillips. Excerpts from their volume, *Weevils in the Wheat: Interviews with Virginia Ex-Slaves*, appear herein with the generous permission of the University Press of Virginia.

In the radio documentary, the written words of former slaves were brought to life by the voices of Debbie Allen, Clifton Davis, Louis Gossett, Jr., James Earl Jones, Melba Moore, Esther Rolle, Jedda Jones, John Sawyer, and host Tonea Stewart. Composer Bryant Pugh provided the extraordinary musical accompaniment.

The radio programs are supported by grants from the National Endowment for the Humanities, the Corporation for Public Broadcasting, the Southern Humanities Media Fund, and the Alabama Humanities Council.

Ira Berlin
Marc Favreau
Steven F. Miller
College Park, Maryland

INTRODUCTION: SLAVERY AS MEMORY AND HISTORY

The struggle over slavery's memory has been almost as intense as the struggle over slavery itself. For many, the memory of slavery in the United States was too important to be left to the black men and women who experienced it directly. The stakes were too great. The American nation had invested much in slavery, maintaining it for more than two centuries and destroying it in a bloody Civil War that took nearly one million lives and destroyed billions of dollars in property. Indeed, its demise elevated slavery's importance and intensified the struggle over how it should be remembered by posterity. Northerners who fought and won the war at great cost incorporated the abolitionists' perspective into their understanding of American nationality: slavery was evil, a great blot that had to be excised to realize the full promise of the Declaration of Independence. At first, even some white Southerners— former slaveholders among them—accepted this view, conceding that slavery had burdened the South as it had burdened the nation and declaring themselves glad to be rid of it. But during the late nineteenth century, after attempts to reconstruct the nation on the basis of equality collapsed and demands for sectional reconciliation mounted, the portrayal of slavery changed. White Northerners and white Southerners began to depict slavery as a benign and even benevolent institution, echoing themes from the planters' defense of the antebellum order. They contrasted the violence and enmity of the postwar period with the supposed tranquility of slave times, when happy slaves frolicked in the service of indulgent masters. Such views, popularized in the stories of Joel Chandler Harris and the songs of Stephen Foster, became pervasive during the first third of the twentieth century.

Against this new romanticized representation of slavery stood the men and women who had survived the institution. Frederick Douglass and other members of the old abolitionist generation railed against the rehabilitation of slavery's reputation, testifying from personal experience to its ugly power. But as death shrank their numbers, the old opponents of slavery could rarely be heard outside the black community. Their frail and distant voices were generally ignored, if heard at all, by the majority of white Americans.

Still, the men and women who survived slavery had much to tell. And as the first generation of black people born in freedom came of age, fears that the slave experience would be lost forever troubled some scholars, particularly those at African-American colleges for whom the new portrayal of slavery was an anathema. At Fisk University in Nashville, Southern University in Baton Rouge, and Kentucky State University in Frankfort, historians initiated projects to interview former slaves. Their accounts, published privately or in the recently established *Journal of Negro History* during the 1920s, had little impact on the larger historical profession. White historians either discounted the validity of these accounts or saw them as peripheral to what they believed to be slavery's larger meaning in American life—its role in the coming of the Civil War. According to historian Ulrich B. Phillips, whose view of slavery as a benign institution dominated the field, the "asseverations of politicians, pamphleteers, and aged survivors" were hopelessly tainted, unfit to use even as a "supplement" to other, superior sources. By and large, the ex-slave narratives of the 1920s languished in the archives unread.

While ignored by historians, the narratives impressed folklorists, whose discipline gained new visibility in the 1930s. The Great Depression forced scholars, like all Americans, to reconsider the experience of the American people. In the study of history, as in many other disciplines, the emphasis was on the common folk, their language, song, art, and stories. The New Deal's Federal Writers' Project—one of several efforts to employ artists, musicians, and actors—gloried in the celebration of everyday Americans. Among its tasks was the collection of first-hand biographies of ordinary American people.

To this end, a special section of the Federal Writers' Project directed first by John A. Lomax, then by Benjamin A. Botkin, and finally by Sterling A. Brown, took up the task that black scholars had begun in the 1920s. Lawrence Reddick of Kentucky State University, who in 1935 had expanded his earlier work into the Ohio Valley under the auspices of Federal Emergency Relief Administration, bridged the work of black scholars and the new, more expansive federal effort. Between 1936 and 1938, project-sponsored interviewers in seventeen states collected the reminiscences of thousands of former slaves. In the process, they produced tens of thousands of pages of typescripts. In some cases, photographs of the interviewees and their families accompanied the documentation. Although the project was terminated before its completion, by the end of the decade some of the interviews were finding their way into print. In 1939, control of the Federal Writers' Project passed from the federal government to the states, and in October of that year the interviews were deposited at the Library of Congress in Washington. There Benjamin Botkin and his staff began evaluating and indexing the interviews, and two years later the "Slave Narratives: A Folk History of Slavery in the United States from Interviews with Former Slaves" was placed in the Library's manuscript room.

Even before the Federal Writers' Project had expanded and extended Reddick's work in the Ohio Valley, another group of scholars had begun to record the words and songs of former slaves. Burdened by primitive recording equipment and the lack of precedents to guide them, these pioneering men and women—who included John and Ruby Lomax and John's son Alan, Zora Neal Hurston, Roscoe Lewis, and John Henry Faulk—journeyed through the South trying to capture the voices of men and women who had experienced slavery. John Lomax, who had just been appointed honorary curator of the Library of Congress's Archive of Folk Song, led the effort; his and his son's work inspired Faulk, who was then beginning his graduate studies at the University of Texas. Others, working separately, followed the same course, often in consultation with Lomax and sometimes with the aid of Rosenwald fellowships. It would be Faulk, whose work extended into the early 1940s, who would eventually make the most important recordings of former slaves. His acetate discs would be deposited in the Library of Congress, where they were incorporated into the Archive of Folk Song, and in the University of Texas Library in Austin.

Historians of slavery continued to ignore this rich trove of evidence, although its existence became well known with the 1945 publication of Benjamin Botkin's *Lay My Burden Down*, the first of many anthologies drawn from the Federal Writers' Project narratives. Indeed, soon after the appearance of Botkin's volume, the Library of Congress microfilmed its collection to increase availability. Still, most historians treated the narratives with disdain. Some scholars condemned them as tainted by the unreliable memories of elderly informants, most of whom had been children at the time of slavery's demise; others questioned the statistical representativeness of the informants, who equaled roughly 2 percent of the ex-slave population in 1930 and, of course, only a tiny fraction of the slave population in 1860. Thus, through the 1950s, the slave narratives gathered dust in federal depositories, and many of those in state archives and private hands may have been destroyed or lost forever.

Beginning in the 1960s, though, stoked by the Civil Rights movement, a growing interest in slavery as the root cause of America's racial dilemma reawakened interest in the narratives. Concerned with slavery less as a cause of the Civil War than as the primary experience of millions of Americans, historians pored over the narratives as a means of gaining access to the slaves' voices. In 1972, when George P. Rawick compiled and published nineteen volumes of the Library of Congress's transcripts under the title *The American Slave: A Composite Autobiography,* he saw as his "primary reason . . . to make it possible to gain a perspective on the slave experience in North America from those who had been slaves." True to Rawick's promise, *The American Slave* immediately sparked a thorough rethinking of African-American captivity and underlay major reinterpretations of slavery by John W. Blassingame, Eugene D. Genovese, Herbert G. Gutman, Lawrence Levine, Leon F. Litwack, Albert J. Raboteau, Thomas L. Webber, and Rawick himself. Meanwhile, new collections of narratives were uncovered in state and local archives and brought to print. In 1977, when Rawick published a second series of twelve volumes drawn from state archives as well as the Library of Congress, the number of narratives in print reached 3,500. Another ten volumes followed over the next two years, including the interviews compiled at Fisk University in the 1920s. Archivists and historians, searching out long-lost transcripts, published compilations reflecting the experience of slaves in particular states. From these volumes came yet others assembled for classroom use. The narratives, once dismissed as historical ephemera, had moved to the center of the study of slavery. By 1979, according to one historiographic review, the narratives were "as widely used as any other single source of data on American slavery."

The new scholars of slavery remained skeptical of the narratives' value, but for different reasons than their predecessors. Whereas Phillips had feared that the narratives would cast doubt on benevolent views of slavery, the revisionists worried that the narratives would foster just such a view of a kindly institution. They observed that the interviewers—nearly all of whom were white Southerners—had tended to select the most obsequious informants, "good Negroes" in the euphemism of the day. Noting that most of those interviewed were old and impoverished in a rigidly segregated society, slavery's new historians suspected that ex-slaves had told not what had actually happened but what their interviewers wanted to hear. After all, many of the interviewers were descended from the same people who had once owned the former slaves and their parents. Moreover, they were employed by a government agency, which led some interviewees to believe that the interviewers might help them obtain pensions, relief, or other benefits.

The interviewers themselves, of course, approached their work with their own beliefs and assumptions about slavery and its aftermath. Like most Americans, they generally accepted the notion that the Civil War had been a tragedy, Reconstruction a great mistake, and slavery as much an ordeal for white people as for black people. Even when the interviewers were sympathetic to the slaves' plight, they frequently patronized their subjects, calling them "uncle" and "aunt" and asking leading questions about sensitive issues of race relations, both historical and contemporary, that informants likely feared to answer straightforwardly. By their person and their approach, such interviewers evoked carefully hedged responses. Black men and women, drawing on a tradition that reached back into slavery, answered in a way that obliged the interviewer. Some interviewees preferred not to dredge up painful memories, much less share them with a white interviewer. Others answered in vague generalities that owed at least as much to their suspicions about the questioners as to the dimness of their recollections. A common pattern was to characterize their own treatment under slavery as benign, while describing that of neighboring slaves as brutal. Although such testimony reflected the fact that master–slave relations varied greatly from place to place, the transference in which former slaves attributed to their neighbors that which had actually happened to them revealed both the complexity of contemporary race relations and the manner in which former slaves believed it necessary to cloak their experiences.

As scholars closely inspected the narratives and the records of the Federal Writers' Project, other problems emerged. They discovered that in preparing what project editors called "ex-slave stories," many interviewers edited the informants' words, eliminating references they found indelicate, implausible, personally objectionable, or ideologically offensive. Moreover, interviewers often altered the dialect as well as the words of their informant—sometimes to make them conform to popular caricatures of "authentic" black speech, sometimes to make them conform to standard English. In any case, the narratives were rarely verbatim transcriptions. As a rule, they were reconstructions of conversations based on notes taken by the interviewer. Most of the narratives might best be considered fair summaries. A few were little more than fabrications, far more indicative of the historical memory and racial attitudes of white Southerners in the 1930s than of the lives of black slaves of the 1850s.

But, for all these and other problems, the corpus of narratives had great historic value. Many of the interviews—particularly those taken by sympathetic interviewers—evoked compelling remembrances of slavery of the sort it is impossible to fabricate. Former slaves were often eager to tell their tales, even to the most condescending of interviewers. Some had lost their fear of retaliation, prefacing their remarks with a warning that their interviewer might not like what they had to say, but they had to speak their minds. Although some interviewers may have dismissed their accounts—a few went so far as to record their displeasure or dissent in footnotes to their transcripts or memos to their superiors—many accepted them. The age of the former slaves, and the respect traditionally granted elderly people in Southern society, often provided an opportunity for slaves to speak openly and forcefully. Moreover, the administrators of the Federal Writers' Project, aware of how the former slaves' testimony was being adulterated, issued directives against such revisions, which restrained some of the more zealous editors and curbed the more outlandish dialect renderings.

Viewed from this perspective, the narratives were like every other historical source: they had strengths and weaknesses. If they were in some respects tainted, so too were other sources of slavery—including the records produced by slaveholders and their white supporters. The historian's task was, as always, to employ them in ways that maximized their utility. The best scholars of slavery have used them critically and cautiously, carefully evaluating the quality of each narrative, verifying the ex-slaves's memory against other sources, and sometimes even sifting through multiple versions of the same interview. Thus, the narratives, have become subject to all the requirements of any other historical source.

While the typescript narratives, readily available in print, became a standard source for the study of slavery, historians gave little attention to the sound recordings of the ex-slaves. During the 1960s, the Archive of Folk

Song at the Library of Congress transferred its recordings from the fragile aluminum and acetate discs to ten-inch tape reels, but the sound remained scratchy and often inaudible; not until the mid 1980s did they attract a group of linguists interested in the evolution of African-American English. Led by Guy Bailey, Natalie Maynor, and Patricia Cukor-Avila, they began to transcribe the sound recordings and, in 1991, their book, *The Emergence of Black English: Text and Commentary*, presented detailed transcriptions of the tapes. Other scholars, most notably Jeutonne P. Brewer of the University of North Carolina, Greensboro, have since developed improved versions.

Linguists found in the recordings an extraordinarily rich opportunity to study the development of Black English Vernacular. Viewing the recordings as primary texts, they not only discovered new ways of understanding the transformation of language in the African-American community but also developed new standards to measure how faithful Federal Writer's Project interviewers had been to their subjects' words. Moreover, during the 1990s, new techniques of digitizing or "remastering" the old aluminum and acetate discs has made a fuller rendition possible and, in some cases, made intelligible material that had previously been incomprehensible. In so doing, they raised new questions about the written typescripts and gave new importance to the voice recordings.

The recordings, like the typescripts, are problematic as historical sources. Their small number made it impossible to view them as statistically representative. While the interviewers, some of them the nation's most experienced folklorists, demonstrated great sensitivity in questioning aged former slaves, they admitted having difficulty gaining access to informants, since white authorities often viewed them as outside agitators. Harassed and threatened, weighted down with bulky and unwieldy equipment, the recorders had limited range. Moreover, since they worked outside the guidelines of the Federal Writers' Project, they had no particular reason or mandate for focusing on slavery, and their informants often preferred to talk about other matters. Indeed, the recordings tell more about the life after emancipation than before it.

Nonetheless, the recorded interviews had great value. The immediacy of the voices of men and women who had experienced enslavement provided listeners a link to a world of slaves and slaveowners—a world often relegated to the distant past. Through the medium of the spoken word, the slaves' memory exploded out of the archives into the here and now.

Understanding the memories that former slaves brought to freedom is enriched by an understanding of slavery's long history. In 1865, when the defeat of the Confederacy and the ratification of the Thirteen Amendment ended slavery in the United States, black people had been captives for almost two hundred and fifty years. Slavery had its origins in violent usurpation: from the beginning, when the first Africans were dragged across the Atlantic, slavery rested on the most extreme forms of coercion. Murders, beatings, mutilations, and humiliations—both petty and great—were an essential, not an incidental, part of chattel bondage. Across the centuries, the history of slavery could be written as a tale of maniacal sadism by the frenzied slaveowners who lashed, traumatized, raped, and killed their slaves, for the list of lurid tales is endless.

But slavery's brutality inhered less in brutish and sadistic outbursts than in the routine, systematic violence slaveowners found necessary to reduce men and women to things. The commonplace, if relentless, character of the violence implicit in slavery revealed itself when Robert "King" Carter, the largest slaveholder in colonial Virginia, calmly petitioned and received permission from the local court to lop off the toes of his runaways; or when William Byrd, the founder of one of America's great families, forced a slave who wet his bed to drink a "pint of piss"; or when Thomas Jefferson carefully calculated that the greatest punishment he could inflict upon an incorrigible fugitive was to sell him away from his kin.

Violence called forth powerful resistance. Slavery's heroes and heroines should no more be forgotten than should the adversity they confronted. While it is easy to celebrate those who stood up to the bullies and faced—or beat—them down, such as Frederick Douglass in his classic confrontation with the slavebreaker Covey, it is equally important to appreciate the silent, everyday heroics of the men and women who stoically took the slaveholders' worst and quietly educated their children to take back piecemeal what the "masters" had appropriated at once. In short, men and women recognizing their inability to overthrow slavery, taught their children how to survive until their moment arrived.

But slavery was more complicated than the sad duet of domination and resistance. New World slavery did not originate in a conspiracy to dishonor, shame, or brutalize Africans—although it did all of those things. The design of the American captivity of African peoples was the extraction of labor. This struggle over labor—which made some people rich and powerful, while degrading and denying the very humanity of others—shaped the history of slavery.

Because slavery was a matter of contested power, it was an ever-changing institution. The lives of slaves were different in 1619, when the first Africans marched down the gangplank at Jamestown, than in 1700, when the Plantation Revolution began; and so, as well, than in 1800, when African-Americans began their Great Migration westward across the Appalachians, or in 1861, when the Civil War began the slaves' long-awaited exodus from bondage. While this long history shaped the memories that black people carried from bondage, the last decades of enslavement figured most prominently for those freed in the great Civil War.

Slavery's last years were among its most complex. At the beginning of the nineteenth century, the great mass of slaves lived along the Atlantic seaboard, cultivated tobacco or rice, and practiced a variety of religious faiths derived from Africa. On the eve of emancipation, most slaves resided in the interior of the South, grew cotton or sugar cane, and professed some variant of Christianity. These massive demographic, economic, and cultural changes combined to reweave the fabric of African-American society. At no time in slavery's two-hundred-and-fifty year history in mainland North America was change greater than in the half century prior to the Civil War.

First and perhaps most important of these transformations was the movement of slaves from the eastern seaboard to the interior of the South. In 1810, more than 80 percent of the slave population resided between the Delaware and Savannah rivers in Maryland, Virginia, and the Carolinas. By the beginning of the Civil War, only one-third of the slave population lived in Maryland, Virginia, and North and South Carolina. Most slaves resided in the lower South—Georgia, Alabama, Mississippi, Louisiana, and the states and territories to the west. Indeed, the slave population was growing fastest on the Arkansas and Texas frontier.

Within the Lower South, slaves were even more concentrated. A ribbon of rich soil that stretched from Georgia to Mississippi—the so-called Black Belt, named for the color of the soil and the people who worked it—became a primary site of African-American life in slavery. A second concentration of slaves could be found along the Mississippi River, especially between Memphis and New Orleans. Although slaves in the Black Belt and Mississippi Valley never predominated to the extent they had in lowcountry Carolina during the eighteenth century—where slaves composed more than 90 percent of the population—they nevertheless made up a substantial majority in these areas.

The movement of some million slaves from the seaboard to the Black Belt and the river bottoms of the interior deeply disrupted the civilization that black people had established in the aftermath of their forced exodus from Africa. During nearly two centuries of settlement along the seaboard, African and African-American slaves had created complex communities, linked by ties of kinship and friendship and resting upon a foundation of shared values and beliefs. Those communities became increasing self-contained with the closing of the trans-Atlantic slave trade, which had ended in the Lower South by constitutional mandate in 1808 and a generation earlier in the Upper South. The westward movement of plantation culture—whether it was driven by individual owners who accompanied their slaves or by professional slave traders—tore that society asunder, exiling hundreds of thousands from their birthplace and traumatizing those who remained. Families and sometimes whole communities dissolved under the pressure of this Second Great Migration.

Changes founded on the seaboard resonated in the interior. Generally, it was the young who were the first to be sent west, since frontier planters needed the muscle of young men and women to clear the land as well as their reproductive capacity to ensure a steadily expanding labor force. On the frontier, slaves—disproportionately children—reconstructed African-American life from the memories of the older seaboard civilization, much as their ancestors had earlier fashioned their lives on the western side of the Atlantic from memories of Africa.

Still, in many ways, the Second Great Migration differed from the first, not only dwarfing it in size but also presenting a distinctive demographic outline. The forced trans-Atlantic migration had been heavily weighted toward men, while men and women moved to the interior of the South in roughly equal numbers. Additionally, Africans who arrived in mainland North America in the seventeenth and eighteenth centuries had differed from one another linguistically and culturally, speaking a variety of languages, practicing a host of different customs, and articulating a variety of different beliefs. They knew little of their owners' language or culture, and what they knew, they knew imperfectly. In the nineteenth century, by contrast, African-Americans who were carried into the interior of the South spoke the same language and shared many elements of an evolving American culture. Differences between African-Americans originating in the Chesapeake and the Carolina lowcountry paled in comparison to differences between Africans derived from the Senegambia and Angola. And if Africans had hardly known anything of the Europeans who had enslaved them, African-Americans knew the ways of their owners all too well.

Whatever the differences between the trans-Atlantic and the trans-Appalachian migrations, the process of cultural reconstruction was similar. Families had to be reconstituted, leadership reasserted, and culture refashioned in new circumstances so that a new generation—one that would know its parents' homeland only through dim recollections—could be tutored in the ways of the elders. In many ways, the memory of Virginia and Carolina—kept alive by the continued influx of newcomers to the west—became as important for black people in the nineteenth-century Black Belt as the memory of Africa had been for black people in the seventeenth- and eighteenth-century seaboard.

The forcible relocation of thousands of African-Americans from the seaboard states also reshaped the lives of those left behind. Slaves who lived under the ever-present threat of sale "down the river" or "to the cotton country" were forced to adjust their hopes and expectations to the relentless reality of the westward movement; in so doing, they reformulated African-American life. Few enslaved parents could expect to nurture their children to maturity, see their grandchildren grow up, or succor their own parents in their last years. Slavery played havoc with African-American family life in the new frontier and the old settlements.

Whatever the effects of the Second Great Migration on Southern slave society at its terminal points, the movement west was neither direct nor linear. Those who traveled west with their owners in family groups or entire plantation populations—rather than with traders in coffles of strangers—enjoyed a measure of security. This was a short-lived consolation, though: few pioneering owners stayed in one spot for long in their search for cheap and fertile land. This process was fueled in part by the Indian removals and government land sales first in Georgia, then in Alabama and Mississippi, and finally in Arkansas and Texas. With little cash and few ties to reliable sources of credit, aspiring planters were vulnerable to the wild swings of a boom-or-bust economy. When catastrophe struck, slaves were ruined with their owners. But even in the best of times, slaves might be sold or traded anywhere along the way, as each stop provided the occasion for yet another division. Separated from friends only recently acquired, many transplanted slaves were forced once again to reconstruct their lives. Among such men, women, and children, for whom transiency was the only certainty, the task of reestablishing shattered ties of kinship and friendship was continual.

The number of slaveholders grew steadily as plantation society marched west. Most newly minted masters and mistresses owned only a few slaves, but most slaves lived on plantations—conventionally defined in the United States as a unit of agricultural production with twenty or more resident slaves. More than one quarter of the slave population—some one million slaves in 1850—dwelled on great plantations with fifty or more slaves. In the states of the Lower South, where the plantations were concentrated, this proportion exceeded one third. Thus, although slaves could be found in a variety of different venues— towns and cities, farmsteads and mill runs, iron forges and turpentine camps—the plantation surpassed all as the locus of nineteenth-century African-American life in slavery.

The plantation was many things, a unit of production and the site of a community, but for slaves plantation life meant work—unrelentingly hard work that began at sunup, paused only slightly at sundown, and frequently continued long into the night. Most plantation slaves engaged in the meanest sort of labor, and they derived few tangible benefits from it. But the same work could also be a source of personal satisfaction and, ultimately, of political self-assertion. The act of creation, which even the most onerous and exploitative labor entailed, allowed slaves to affirm the humanity that chattel bondage denied. By producing something where once there was nothing, slaves discredited the masters' shibboleth that they were simply property, countered the daily humiliations that tested their self-esteem, and laid claim—if only symbolic claim—to the fruits of their labor for themselves and their posterity.

Labor became the terrain on which slaves and their owners battled for the wealth that the slaves produced. The conflict took many forms, involving the organization of labor, the pace of work, the division of labor, and the composition of the labor force. If slaveowners wielded the lash—for slavery never ceased to rest upon brute force—slaves employed an array of weapons of their own, feigning ignorance, slowing the pace, maiming animals, breaking tools, disappearing at critical moments, and, as a last resort, confronting slave owners directly and violently.

The character of these workplace struggles rested, to a considerable degree, on the productive processes themselves, which differed throughout the South. Here, too, much changed between the colonial and the antebellum periods, as many slaveholders abandoned the great staples of the colonial era and introduced new ones. During the seventeenth and eighteenth centuries, most plantation slaves grew tobacco and rice, with indigo being a secondary crop in lowcountry Carolina and in Louisiana. While the cultivation of tobacco and rice remained important in the nineteenth-century South—indigo fell to the vagaries of international politics and trade—the crops that plantation slaves grew changed. The American government's purchase of Louisiana during the first decade of the nineteenth century placed a major sugar-producing area within the bounds of the United States. Many planters, particularly in the Upper South, grew less tobacco and expanded cereal production. They introduced new crops such as hemp, and new varieties of older ones such as bright-leafed tobacco, all the while diversifying their output by combining traditional crops with dairying and herding.

Each of the great staples had evolved a particular regimen, which both reflected and shaped the demography, economy, and society of the region in which it was grown. Around the Chesapeake, for example, slaves grew tobacco on independent satellite farms called "quarters," which were organized around a single large estate. At the home quarter, resident planters presided over what observers characterized as small villages with the Great House nestled among artisan shops, barns, an ice house, laundry, and occasionally even a small infirmary—buildings denominated, with a nice sense of the plantation's social order, as "dependencies." Rice, on the other hand, was produced on larger unitary plantations carved out the swamps of the South Carolina and Georgia lowlands. Production was directed by planters residing in Savannah, Charleston, or the lesser rice ports rather than on site, through a long chain of command at the base of which stood slave foremen or "drivers." In southern Louisiana, sugar production presented yet another spatial and organizational schema. Estates encompassed both agricultural production and industrial processing—the fields in which the cane was grown and the mill in which it was transformed into sugar and molasses. Farm and factory surrounded the Great House, whose owner typically also spent much time in a New Orleans or Natchez townhouse.

The diverse economic geography of plantation life reflected an equally diverse occupational structure, managerial hierarchy, and work regimen. Although sugar was grown by large gangs of field hands supervised by white overseers, it required a small army of slave artisans to process the cane, pack the sugar and molasses into hogsheads, and transport them by wagon and boat. Rice planters, operating from their urban command posts, eschewed gang labor and instead organized fieldwork by the "task," thereby allowing slaves to set the pace of their labor and giving them a small measure of time to work independently for their own benefit. Tobacco planters, preoccupied with care of the broad-leafed weed—the tedious process of worming, topping, suckering, and priming through the summer until the mature plant was cut, stripped, cured, and packed in hogsheads in the winter—organized their slaves in closely supervised squads rather than gang-sized units.

The organization of tobacco, rice, and sugar production—as well as that of wheat and other small grains—had been established in the eighteenth century. But it did not remain unaltered in the new era. Alert to agricultural reform, planters throughout the South introduced new tools, experimented with new work regimens, and inaugurated new systems of management in an effort to squeeze more profit from their slaves' labor. The introduction of new technology, new methods, and new systems of supervision set in motion new conflicts between slave owners and slaves, keeping the plantation in perpetual turmoil.

Yet no tool or method had as powerful an effect on nineteenth-century slave life as the changes set in motion by the Cotton Revolution. Few mainland slaves grew cotton prior to American independence. This changed dramatically in the last decade of the eighteenth century, as the first stirring of the Industrial Revolution increased demand for the fiber. Along the Georgia and Carolina coast, planters quickly expanded production of long-staple cotton, whose smooth black seeds were easily separated by hand from its luxuriant, silky strands. But this variety grew well only in the unique environs of the lowcountry South Carolina and

Georgia, and attempts to expand production of a short-staple variety were hindered by the difficulty of removing its sticky green seeds from the fiber. Once that obstacle was overcome by the invention of a mechanical "gin," though, production soared, and cotton cultivation spread quickly to the uplands east of the Appalachians and then across the mountains to the newly opened territories of Tennessee, Alabama, and Mississippi. By 1820, cotton production had moved west into the interior of the South, sinking its deepest roots in the Black Belt.

The creation of the vast empire of cotton was the work of a generation of slaves, who cleared the land, broke the soil, "chopped" (or thinned out) the young cotton plants, picked the tufts of fiber from the prickly bolls, separated the seeds from the fiber, packed the fiber into bales, and sent it off to manufacture in Europe or the North. In 1800, the South produced less than one hundred thousand bales of cotton; sixty years later, cotton production stood at over four million bales—the vast majority of which was grown by slaves. On the eve of the Civil War, some three million slaves—three-quarters of the Southern slave population— were directly involved in the production of cotton.

Because cotton was grown almost everywhere in the Lower South, and parts of the Upper South as well, and because its cultivation occupied the vast majority of slaves, its special requirements and seasonal rhythms shaped the development of slave culture. Its most distinguishing characteristic was utter simplicity of production and the general absence of supporting crafts. Unlike sugar, whose production was equally industrial and agricultural, or even tobacco and rice, cotton, once ginned, required almost no refining or special handling. Virtually imperishable so long as it was kept dry, cotton needed no packing in barrels or housing in specially designed barns or sheds. Squeezed into bales by a simple mechanical process, it could sit under a tarpaulin on a plantation landing or in an urban warehouse for months or even years. Consequently, the occupational structure of the cotton plantation lacked the diversity and complexity of estates devoted to tobacco, rice, or sugar. With the exception of a blacksmith or carpenter on a great plantation, virtually all slaves were field hands who did pretty much the same work. The slave coopers, wheelwrights, harness-makers, and tanners who serviced the plantation economy during the eighteenth century, and whose presence was so visible on the great sugar estates in the nineteenth century, were almost totally absent from cotton plantations. Cotton planters sometimes promoted a particularly adept slave to the head of a work gang in the hope that he or she would set a fast pace; or sometimes they distinguished between field workers who plowed and those who hoed. In general, though, the uniformity of the processes associated with planting, cultivating, and harvesting cotton reduced the significance of such a division of labor to differences of age and sex. The movement from seaboard to the interior, from tobacco and rice to cotton, occasioned a sharp decline of skilled slaves.

Moreover, since there was no special urgency in moving cotton to market and since the Lower South was a particularly well-watered region with plantations often located by a river or bayou, wagoners—along with blacksmiths, wheelwrights, harness-makers, and tanners who served them—were also much reduced in number. As boatmen and wagoners disappeared from the plantation roster, the number of slaves who regularly traversed the countryside and thereby gained knowledge of the world beyond the plantation also declined.

The growth of cotton culture also reduced the proportion of slaves—almost always men—in managerial positions. In the eighteenth century, urban-based rice planters relied upon drivers to mediate between themselves and their plantation slaves. In the Chesapeake, tobacco planters frequently placed trusted slaves in charge of individual quarters. Indeed, many quarters took the name of the slave foreman. While slave drivers and foremen continued to reign in the older plantation areas, they were far less common in the cotton South, where the white overseer became a plantation fixture. Thus, as cotton came to dominate Southern agriculture, the prospects for social mobility, like those for geographical mobility, declined.

The Cotton Revolution altered slave life in still other ways. Slaveholding planters seized control of rich soils of the Black Belt and the river basins, relegated yeoman farmers to the margins, and dominated the production of the staple. However, cotton plantations rarely grew so large, or became so profitable, as to support the quasi-absenteeism of either rice or sugar production, where slaveowners maintained an urban residence at least part of the year. Only a few cotton planters could afford to single out more than one or two adult slaves for special duties in the house. Indeed, most house servants were children. Those adults who worked in and around the Big House often labored in the field part of the time; or if they did not, they had kinfolks and friends who did. The distance between house and field in the cotton South was small— physically and socially—and slaves moved easily between the Big House and the quarter.

The few slave men and women who had a permanent place in the Big House as cooks and carriage drivers, seamstresses and valets, housekeepers and gardeners had little opportunity to pass their special place in the plantation hierarchy to their children. Such a hereditary class had begun to emerge in the seaboard South during the late eighteenth century, as planters elaborated their great estates. The movement west severed these lines of occupational descent, and the advent of cotton culture stymied their reformation. The absence of a hereditary retinue of house servants or a corps of body servants in the cotton South, like the absence of a large number of plantation-based tradesmen and managers, promoted solidarity within the slave community, creating an intraplantation unity that was unique among the plantation slaves of the New World.

With the resident planter as its beau ideal, life on the plantation became increasingly insular during the nineteenth century. Planters sealed the borders of their estates and claimed the right to regulate visitors to the quarter. They denounced marriages outside of the plantation "family" and became chary about slaves traveling off the plantation for any reason. Such practices had been common in the eighteenth-century seaboard South and continued into the nineteenth century in the Upper South, where the small size of agricultural units made visiting and interplantation marriages a necessity. To curb the mobility of their slaves, some planters constructed their labor force in a manner calculated to provide every marriageable hand a partner within the estate. A few even purchased slaves for this reason. Planters were never entirely successful in closing their estates to the outside world, as patterns of sociability and the necessity of production continued to breach the barriers they tried to create. Nonetheless, plantation borders became considerably less permeable in the nineteenth century than they had been in the eighteenth, and slave society became more insular as a result. If relocation from one estate to another became an increasingly common experience, once relocated the slaves' acquaintance with the world outside their residence shrank.

Within the boundaries of the plantation, Southerners—both black and white—came to identify themselves with the land, its singular beauty, and its ancient mysteries. Although the reality of Southern life belied this image of ageless stability, slaveholding planters found much to like in this seeming timelessness. From it, they inferred an immutable relationship between subordinate and superior.

Planters understood this relationship in terms of the patriarchal ideal. Emphasizing that their slaves, like their wives and children, were fed and clothed out of the household larder, slaveholders celebrated their special responsibility for the workers they owned, whom they often called "family." Planters draped themselves in the cloak of paterfamilias and consigned their slaves to an eternal childhood, often denominating them "girls" and "boys" until age had transformed them into "uncles" and "aunts." The slaveholders' assault fell particularly heavily on slave men: equating manhood with control over an independent household, the masters of the great plantation contested their right to choose a wife, discipline their children, and care for their aged parents, thus relegating slave men to a lesser roles within their own families.

The incorporation of slaves into what planters called their "family, white and black" enhanced the slaveholders' sense of responsibility for their slaves and encouraged the owners to improve the material circumstances of plantation life. Slaves were generally better fed and housed in the nineteenth century than they had been in the seventeenth and eighteenth. Along with these material improvements, however, came a deepening intrusion into the private portions of life in the quarter. Aspects of slave life that slaveholders had largely ignored during the eighteenth-century—everything from child-rearing to religious practices—came under intense scrutiny during the nineteenth, as owners became increasingly self-conscious about their patriarchal responsibilities. Still, like all ideologues, slaveholders violated their own principles when it suited their purposes; and, like all paternalists, slaveholders tended to emphasize their subordinates' responsibility to them rather than their responsibility to their subordinates. Indeed, the paternalist ideology provided slaveholders with a powerful justification for their systematic expropriation of the slaves' labor.

Slaves viewed relations with their owners from a different perspective. Though subject to their owners' overwhelming power, slaves struggled to increase their independence in all areas of their lives, asserting that in every way they were full human beings. They pressed for nothing more relentlessly than control over their own labor, the denial of which constituted the very essence of chattel slavery. Conceding what they could not alter or deny, slaves worked without direct compensation but claimed a right to a predictable portion of what they produced. They expected their owners to feed, clothe, and house them in accordance with customary usage. Challenging their owners to meet their paternalist ideal, slaves insisted that "good masters" provided well materially for their slaves; but, while they welcomed the regular allotment of rations and played their part in the charade surrounding Christmas gifting, they did not rest satisfied with the dole.

Through a continuous process of contest and negotiation with slaveholders—often playing on the slaveholders' recognition of their humanity implicit in paternal ideology—slaves established the right to control a portion of their lives. When permitted to do so, they used small grants of free time to cultivate gardens, hunt, and fish; raise poultry, pigs, and cattle; make baskets, weave clothes, and practice other handicrafts; hire themselves to neighboring farmers and artisans; and receive payments for overwork. Although the property they accumulated had no legal standing, it gained recognition in practice. The slaves' self-directed economic activities—what historians have called "the slaves' economy"—fostered a vision of an independent life, even though the opportunity to realize the vision would not come until after emancipation.

The Second Great Migration and the Cotton Revolution threatened to unravel the customs that had been established through a long process of hard bargaining and continuous struggle. Access to gardens and provision grounds, free Sundays and half Saturdays, the right to visit friends, market produce, and keep small earnings from work done outside the owners' ken were all put at risk by the creation of a new plantation order.

Slaveholders used the new circumstance of life and labor in the interior and the isolation of transplanted slaves to ratchet up labor demands. They increased time spent in the field and expanded the stint or the task for which slaves were responsible, reduced the slaves's free time and cut the number of holidays, denied the right to travel off the plantation, and constricted the slaves' internal economy. Although the new circumstances of the interior sometimes offered slaves new opportunities to limit the authority of the owner, generally it was the master who gained from starting afresh. Indeed, many slaveholders saw in the movement west an opportunity to liquidate the limits slaves had set and to begin plantation life anew. Customary practices established in years of hard bargaining withered in the shadow of the Second Great Migration and dissolved in the heat of the Cotton Revolution.

Against the slaveholders' assault, slaves drew upon their memory of the past and an array of institutions they had created for their own benefit. The most important of these was the African-American family. Since the early eighteenth century, African and African-American slaves in mainland North America had been a population growing by natural increase, with births exceeding deaths. Slaveowners, who were often marginal to the larger Atlantic plantation system, seized upon the prospect of this self-reproducing labor force and turned from the trans-Atlantic slave trade to natural growth as a source of labor. By the late eighteenth century, the growth of an indigenous African-American slave population allowed mainland slaveholders to close the African trade or acquiesce to the 1808 Constitutional mandate to end it.

Playing upon the slaveholders' dependence on the slaves' natural increase, slaves struggled for control of the reproductive processes. They asserted the right to choose their marriage partner and control the birthing process. Slave women, or elderly "grannies," served as midwives; only rarely, and then in dire emergencies, did slaveholders and their agents usher slave infants into the world. Slaves challenged their owners' right to name their children, so that while a slaveholder might claim symbolic paternity for the entire plantation family, many children were named after their natural fathers and mothers and only a few named after their owners.

During the nineteenth century, the hallmark of the slave's domestic life was a nuclear family enmeshed in a dense network of kin relationships. Courting and sexual activity between young slave men and women began in their late teens. Sometimes these relations begot children, but Southern slaves generally did not marry until their early twenties, when they settled down in long-term monogamous relationships, which generally lasted until disruption by sale or death. Although women bore primary responsibility for child care, the slave family was not a matriarchy, and men played an important and visible role in supporting their households, raising children, and, on occasion, protecting wives and children from the overwhelming power of the master and his underlings.

A web of distinctive customs and beliefs sustained those lifelong relations and separated the family life of African-American slaves from that of other Southerners. For example, nineteenth-century slaves rarely married blood relatives. Indeed, marriage between slaves as distantly connected as second cousins was so unusual as to suggest the existence of a powerful proscription that some scholars have traced back to Africa. Such endogamy distinguished slaves from their owners (as well as from propertied free people of color) who regularly married within much closer blood relations. Indeed, cousin marriage was one of the distinguishing features of the domestic life of the planter class.

Although usually known to their owners by only a single name, most slaves in fact had surnames or, as they called them, "titles," which they maintained clandestinely. Titles stretched back to Africa on occasion, but more commonly slaves reached for the most distant genealogical marker they could identify, perhaps the name of their forebears' first owner. Slave surnames, although derived from the owning class, distinguished the slaves who adopted them from their present owner and established—at least in their own eyes—a separate lineage, heritage, and identity that contested the masters' claims to rule a "family, white and black."

Slaves nurtured these generational connections in violation of laws that denied their existence. Slaves who had accumulated small amounts of property covertly developed their own system of inheritance, whereby one generation of slaves gave the next "a start." These inheritance practices differed from place to place, but they became more deeply entrenched as slaves elaborated their internal economies. Although the property passed from generation to generation was often nothing more than a few sticks of furniture, some cookware and tools, or a few barnyard animals, generational exchanges had deep emotive and psychological meaning. And they were not without material significance.

Scarcely less important than the family was the slaves' religion. Whereas the dense network of kinship that knit together the slave community in the nineteenth century had evolved along lines established in the seventeenth and eighteenth centuries, the religion of the quarter emerged from a new set of circumstances. Prior to American independence, most slaves knew little of Christianity, and most slaveholders were indifferent if not hostile to their slaves imbibing the teaching of Jesus. Despite the efforts of missionary organizations, few slaves converted to Christianity, and most remained unchurched. However, a series of evangelical awakenings that began prior to the American Revolution and continued into the nineteenth century changed that radically. To the evangelicals, nothing more fully validated the power of God's grace than the conversion of the lowly slave. Indeed, some evangelical Christians not only welcomed slaves into the fold as brothers and sisters in Christ but also openly criticized slavery and, on occasion, accepted the leadership of black preachers and ministers.

The egalitarianism of these evangelical revivals waned in the late eighteenth century and had been all but extinguished among slaveholders by the first decade of the nineteenth century. Nevertheless, many slaveholders remained committed to converting their slaves—not so much as Christian egalitarians seeking a unity in Christ but as Christian stewards bringing their God to heathens and slaveholding paternalists bringing their civilization to savages. That the promise of a better life in the afterworld might make for greater subordination of slaves in the present made this new missionary spirit that much more compelling to some members of the slaveholding class. Drawing upon the Pauline dictum that slaves should obey their masters, slaveholders built plantation chapels, invited itinerant ministers to preach to their slaves, and—donning the paternalist mantle—sometimes led their slaves in prayer and Bible catechism.

For their part, slaves were increasingly receptive to the possibility of joining their owner's church. For some, it assured a Sabbath respite from labor and an occasion for fellowship with other slaves from neighboring plantations. But it also was an opportunity to practice a religion which, by the story of Moses, promised liberation from earthly bondage and, by the story of Jesus, promised eternal redemption and divine justice, in which the good would be rewarded and the wicked punished.

During the nineteenth century, tens of thousands of slaves converted to Christianity, and many thousands more were born into a faith their eighteenth-century forebears either had not known or had consciously rejected. In its polity, the slaves' new religion did not differ markedly from that of their owners. Most slaves subscribed to Baptist, Methodist, or Presbyterian denominations, although Episcopalian and Lutheran slaves were scattered throughout the South and Catholics abounded in

Louisiana and parts of Maryland and Florida. Seated in the back rows and balconies of their owners' churches, nineteenth-century slaves followed faiths familiar to their owners.

Yet if they shared church buildings, polity, and a variety of religious rituals with their owners, the slaves' religious beliefs and practices nevertheless stood apart. Slaves incorporated Christianity into the diverse African religious practices—some of them polytheistic, some of them Islamic, and some of them pretransfer Christian—that had evolved during the first two hundred years of American captivity into a religion that was itself an amalgam undergoing profound change. The genesis of African-American Christianity was as much the creation of a new faith as the expansion of the white man's religion.

Slaveowners meted out Christianity in carefully measured portions, but slaves were equally selective about what they accepted and how they incorporated it into their view of this world and the next. Patience in the face of earthly trial and obedience to earthly masters loomed large in the slaveholders' message, but slaves found other themes more to their liking. Theologically, they had little truck with the doctrines of Paul and, instead, maintained the egalitarianism of the eighteenth-century revivals, emphasizing the equality of mankind before God and the irrelevance of earthly status to one's chance for eternal life. They identified particularly with the people of the Old Testament and their heroic exodus from bondage. The message of the fundamental equality of all in the eyes of God and—when the master was out of range—in the eyes of man remained a central tenet of African-American Christianity long after it had ceased to echo in the slaveholder's church. But the theology of the black church did more than affirm the slaves' humanity and their worth before God: it envisioned a day of judgment, a "settling-up time" accompanied by a rebalancing of the moral scales.

So too with the theme of salvation, a flexible metaphor that joined earthly liberation and otherworldly redemption. Slave preachers presented the message of salvation skillfully so that, depending on the standpoint of the listener, it could be understood as either deeply conservative of the slave regime or utterly subversive of it. "Free At Last" could speak both to the release from earthy tribulations and the release from chattel bondage. The meaning of the message received by the congregants emerged from the antiphonal repartee of preacher and his flock. It was communicated by gesture and emphasis, long-winded biblical exegeses and significant silences. Because it depended as much on unstated assumptions as on stated doctrine, onlookers, particularly the masters, found it all but inaccessible.

African-American Christianity as it evolved in the nineteenth century thus had many parts, and slaves made use of all of them. Although Christian slaves drew strength from those elements that distinguished their religion from that of their white co-worshippers, they often found it useful to underline the similarities. Just as slaveholders cited the Bible to enjoin their slaves to obedience, slaves did the same, holding their owners accountable to the ethical standards embedded in the Ten Commandments, the Beatitudes, and the Sermon on the Mount.

The domestic and spiritual life of African-American slaves reflected the conflicting and contradictory evolution of the relationship between slaveholders and slaves in the antebellum years. Slaves found glimmerings of independence in the same domestic and religious institutions wherein slaveowners saw confirmation of the slaves' acquiescence to their rule. Indeed, what slaveholders often took as justification of their domination became a source of self-assertion for slaves and the basis of opposition to the masters' hegemony. What was true of family and church was equally true of art, cuisine, dance, language, and other cultural forms. African-American and European-American culture were connected in ways that belied the shifting balance of power between master and slave.

After 1861, when the long-simmering struggle between North and South bubbled over into civil war, the balance shifted sharply, if slowly, in the slaves' favor. Tossing aside the pronouncements of President Abraham Lincoln and other Union leaders that the conflict was a war for national unity, slaves put their own freedom and that of their posterity at the top of the national agenda. Steadily, as opportunities arose, slaves risked all for freedom. By fleeing from their owners, coming uninvited into Union lines, and offering their assistance as laborers, laundresses, cooks, and spies, slaves forced federal soldiers at the lowest level to recognize their importance to the Union's success. In time, that understanding ascended the chain of command. Eventually even the most obdurate federal commanders and policymakers came to appreciate that salvation of the Union depended on the destruction of slavery. In the summer of 1862, the U.S. Congress and President Lincoln sanctioned the exchange of freedom for military labor in the federal cause. By then, some Union generals were envisioning a more direct military role for slaves. They began to enlist slave men as soldiers, against the direct orders of their superiors. Those orders would soon change. On January 1, 1863, Lincoln's Emancipation Proclamation declared free all slaves within the Confederate states, announced the federal army's intention to recruit black men as soldiers, and officially transformed the war for Union into a war for liberty. By war's end, more than 200,000 black men, most of them former slaves, had served in the federal army and navy, whose steady advance brought freedom to an ever-larger portion of the slave population. Following the end of the war, the Thirteenth Amendment to the Constitution ended slavery forever.

From the start, the former slaves' recollections of slavery focused on the last years of the institution. The great events that had propelled them to freedom amid the tumult of Civil War loomed large. The last generation